Class - 1 000 rooms

Fe by the Rio Grande, Hotel Cheyenne
the Far West. A Wild West scene has been
ambling amidst brightly painted buildings.
its and ask yourself what else might have
er, you might even run into some trigger-
y Fort Apache, the covered wagons and

...eet, the main street with a name that says it all, runs right through the centre of town. The buildings on either side (with names such as Jesse James, Calamity Jane and Billy the Kid) contain rooms suitably decorated in the Western style.

In the Red Garter Saloon, drinks are served to an accompaniment of Country and Western music.

There is a free bus service to the theme park and *Festival Disney*.

Hotel Santa Fe

Economy Class - 1 000 rooms

A drive-in cinema screen marks the entrance. The hotel's theme is the American Southwest and especially New Mexico with its arid climate and sun-parched soil.

Forty or so pueblos, painted in subdued desert colours, are laid out in four groups or trails, which abound in symbolic reference to the history and mythology of New Mexico; one of these trails has a volcano, dormant for the moment...

Children will particularly enjoy the themed playground known as Totem Circle and the *Pow Wow* games room.

There is a free bus service to the theme park and *Festival Disney*.

Davy Crockett Ranch

The woods of Citry are the attractive setting for this campsite (56ha-139 acres). It is divided into two distinct areas: one is set aside for camping and caravanning; the other contains fully-equipped cabins that can accommodate four to six people. The Alamo Trading Post sells groceries and sundries.

Among the many recreational facilities offered are: indoor swimming pool, tennis courts, sports grounds (football, basketball, etc), bicycle rental and horse or pony rides.

Do not be surprised to see two forest friends – Chip'n'Dale.

Liberty Court

As part of Liberty Arcade, Liberty Court pays homage to "the grandest lady in the world" – the Statue of Liberty – who has welcomed travellers to New York Harbour for more than a hundred years.

This special exhibit and tableau depicts the **Statue of Liberty's** inauguration ceremony, held on the 28 October 1886, in the presence of the American President, Grover Cleveland, and French sculptor Auguste Bartholdi.

✓ La Parade Disney★★

More than 200 actors and actresses take part in this colourful musical carnival parade through the park every day. The procession is headed by Mickey and Minnie Mouse in a plane, followed by a dozen or so magnificently decorated floats accompanied by other Disney characters and dancers. Each float has a Disney film as its theme, so keep your eyes open for familiar faces (Sleeping Beauty, Pinocchio, Snow White, Cinderella, Dumbo, Peter Pan, Mowgli, Roger Rabbit, the Little Mermaid, Beauty and the Beast, Aladdin and Princess Jasmine)!

✓ Main Street Electrical Parade★★

After nightfall, at certain times of the year, a procession of lights wends its way through the park.

Beautifully decorated floats representing the wonderful world of Disney create a fairylike scene as they proceed up Main Street and through Fantasyland.

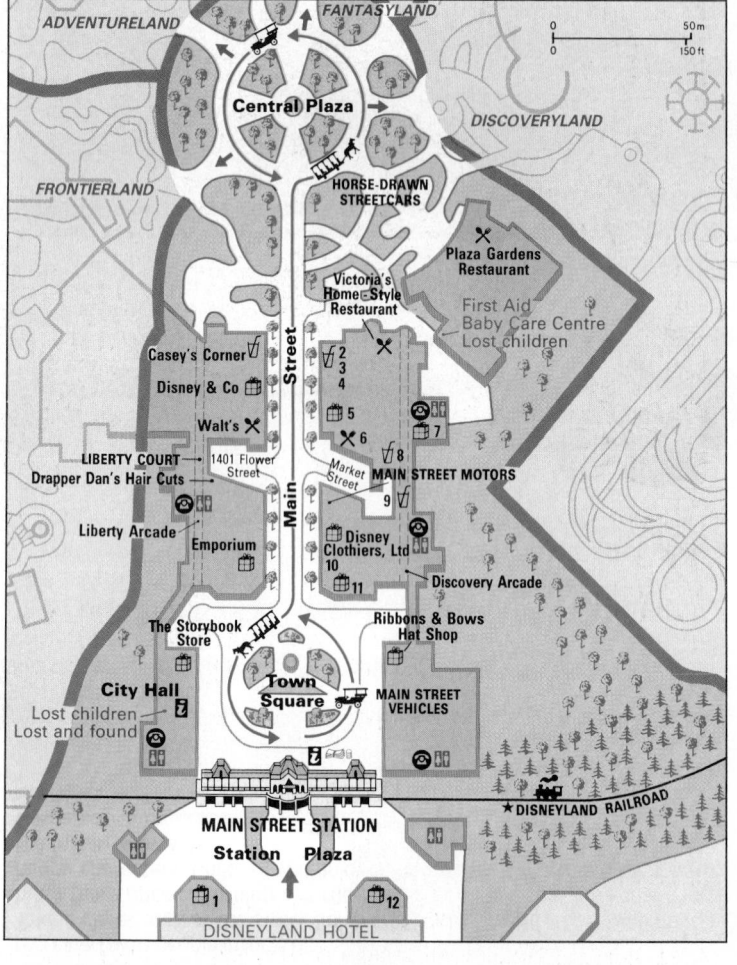

1 Plaza West Boutique – **2** The Gibson Girl Ice Cream Parlour – **3** Cookie Kitchen
4 Cable Car Bake Shop – **5** Harrington's Fine China & Porcelains
6 Market House Deli – **7** Disneyana Collectibles – **8** The Coffee Grinder
9 The Ice Cream Company – **10** Boardwalk Candy Palace

Disneyland
PARIS

MICHELIN ®

46, av. de Breteuil - 75324 PARIS CEDEX 07 / 38 Clarendon Road - WATFORD Herts WD1 1SX

Childhood Friends

Only the main characters invented by Walt Disney are described below. Others, like Snow White, Peter Pan, Winnie the Pooh or Pinocchio, are taken from well-known fairy tales or stories.

Mickey Mouse

He is undoubtedly Walt Disney's most famous creation. The amiable mouse imagined by Walt Disney and drawn by his friend, Ub Iwerks, came into being in 1928. He was originally to be called Mortimer but his name was changed to Mickey to please Walt's wife, Lillian.

Mickey was first animated in a film called *Plane Crazy*, inspired by aviator Charles Lindbergh's historic non-stop crossing of the Atlantic the previous year.

On 18 November, Mickey Mouse made his screen début as Steamboat Willie, and, in 1930, he became the hero of a comic strip. In 1940, Walt Disney gave him the part of the Sorcerer's Apprentice in *Fantasia*. To Paul Dukas's impetuous orchestral score, Mickey donned his famous pointed hat and cast his spells. Mickey Mouse's fame spread worldwide; his name became inseparable from that of Walt Disney.

Mickey Mouse is everyone's friend, standing for courage, honesty, loyalty and intelligence.

Minnie Mouse

Mickey's girlfriend came to life in 1928 in the cartoon *Steamboat Willie*. Singer, dancer and actress, she is a frequent associate and adviser in Mickey's adventures.

Pluto

Pluto first appeared in a cartoon in 1930. He is a good-natured hound with droopy ears, that can shoot straight up on occasion.

He is Mickey Mouse's faithful companion, credulous, brave up to a point, sentimental and obliging.

The Three Little Pigs and the Big Bad Wolf

They were first the subject of a *Silly Symphony* (see Walt Disney A Life Devoted to Enchantment below) in 1933 which earned Walt Disney his second Academy Award. The theme tune is hummed the world over. **Fiddler Pig** and **Fifer Pig**, both carefree, and **Practical Pig**, a serious-minded mason, must forever be wary of the **Big Bad Wolf** whose sole ambition is to gobble them up. His son **Little Wolf** is very gentle-natured, unlike his dad, and friend to the Three Little Pigs. Little Wolf first appeared in the cartoon

Each hotel room can accommodate up to 4 people and has a separate bathroom, colour television, telephone and a minibar (except in Hotels Cheyenne and Santa Fé).

A number of hotels have facilities for receptions, banquets, conferences and ballroom dances.

Lake Disney offers boating facilities (*"Toobies" and pedalos for hire from the Marina del Rey, Festival Disney*). A landscaped promenade around the lake edge connects the various hotels, to the entertainment centre, Festival Disney, and the Disneyland Paris theme park.

In addition to the six hotels and the campsite there is an entertainment centre (Festival Disney) and a 27-hole golf course.

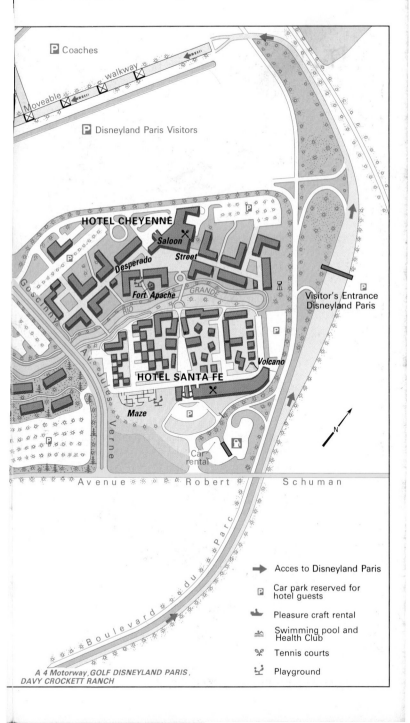

Disneyland Paris

Encircled by its very own "green belt", the Disneyland Paris theme park, similar to Florida's Magic Kingdom, consists of five themed lands each with its own unique appearance: Main Street, U.S.A.; Frontierland; Adventureland; Fantasyland and Discoveryland. Covering more than 55ha - 136 acres, the theme park offers attractions, live entertainment, restaurants and shops.

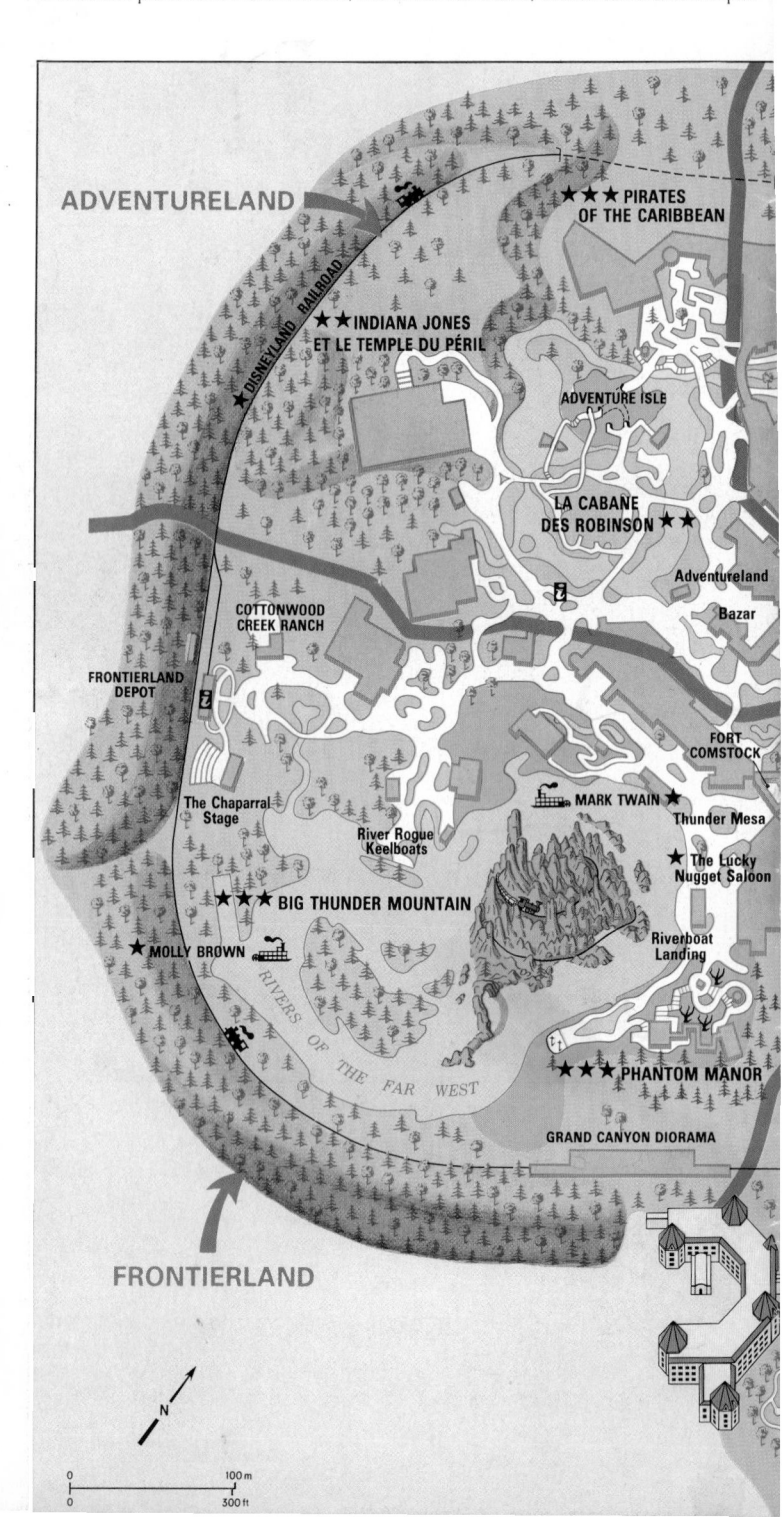

ADVENTURELAND

★★★ PIRATES OF THE CARIBBEAN

DISNEYLAND RAILROAD

★★INDIANA JONES ET LE TEMPLE DU PÉRIL

ADVENTURE ISLE

LA CABANE DES ROBINSON ★★

Adventureland Bazar

COTTONWOOD CREEK RANCH

FRONTIERLAND DEPOT

FORT COMSTOCK

The Chaparral Stage

River Rogue Keelboats

MARK TWAIN ★

Thunder Mesa

★ The Lucky Nugget Saloon

★★★ BIG THUNDER MOUNTAIN

★ MOLLY BROWN

RIVERS OF THE FAR WEST

Riverboat Landing

★★★ PHANTOM MANOR

GRAND CANYON DIORAMA

FRONTIERLAND

N

0   100 m
0   300 ft

Frontierland

The untamed wilderness of the American West comes to life in Thunder Mesa, a re-creation of an old western mining town, complete with cowboys, Indians, gold prospectors, wooden sidewalks, a saloon, and a deserted "ghostly" manor house. A broad waterway **(Rivers of the Far West)** *flows lazily past a large island, from which rises Big Thunder Mountain, inspired by the rock formations found in Monument Valley (located in Arizona and Utah). Next to it, a few trees dot* **Wilderness Island,** *a small uninhabited island.*

Fort Comstock

In this famous US Cavalry fort, a display on **Legends of the Far West** evokes some of the more famous characters and episodes in the history of the Far West (waxworks in reconstructed settings).

Phantom Manor★★★

A gloomy-looking Victorian-style mansion set in eery surroundings overlooks Thunder Mesa. In days gone by, it was the prosperous home to a family who had struck it rich during the Gold Rush. The dilapidated state of the house, with decrepit window frames and crooked shutters, gives the impression that the place is totally deserted. But, you never know.

Pass through a forgotten and overgrown garden to the front door and into the hallway; a voice from the dead invites you to step in and look around – spine-chilling but tempting all the same. Now it is too late to turn back; the front door has closed as if by magic; the walls begin to stretch.

Small black carriages take you on a journey that will make your hair stand on end. The ghostly special effects are remarkable.

Strange-looking tombstones in the derelict family graveyard, Boot Hill, bring to memory those who have passed away.

D. Hée/MICHELIN

Big Thunder Mountain★★★

This unusual mountain, with a mine hollowed out of its side, seems worth exploring. While waiting for the **train,** visitors should examine the authentic mining and hoisting equipment, a coal furnace, a mule pen…

The train takes a tunnel under the river, arrives at the mountain and that is where the thrills begin; you are now on a runaway mine train which hurtles out of control through sloping curves, down steep dips and up sharp inclines, amid explosions, rock slides and bats screeching overhead.

Thunder Mesa Riverboat Landing

From the landing stage in the town of Thunder Mesa, two superb steam-powered **riverboats★**, the *Mark Twain* and the *Molly Brown*, cruise peacefully along the Rivers of the Far West through the varied natural scenery in

© Disney

Festival Disney

Entertainment Centre

Polished steel columns (the tallest are 20m-66ft) tower over the vast entertainment centre (it covers some 18 000m²- 2 150sq yds). Its shops, restaurants and discotheque provide a lively glimpse of the American way of life. A variety of street artistes – jugglers, musicians, tightrope walkers, characters on stilts – captivate passers-by. In the evening the centre is bathed in twinkling lights.

The dinner show, **Buffalo Bill's Wild West Show★★**, recalls the Far West with its herds of bison, longhorn cattle, daring equestrian feats, stage-coach hold-up and Indian camp.

Golf Disneyland Paris

The undulating fairways feature bunkers and cascades offering fine sport to the golfer on this 27-hole golf course. The course includes a putting green shaped like Mickey Mouse's head.

The Club House, with a roof shaped like a golf ball, houses a restaurant and a shop.

The holiday resort

Disneyland Paris is a unique kind of holiday resort to Europe. It is designed for short or long stays and has a wide range of accommodation facilities and leisure activities.

The Disneyland Paris hotel complex includes six hotels (three on the banks of Lake Disney, two beside the Rio Grande and Disneyland Hotel near the entrance to the theme park) with a capacity of 5 200 rooms and a campsite (Davy Crockett Ranch) with 97 pitches and 498 cabins.

The architecture, landscaping and cuisine of each hotel are in keeping with those of a particular region in the United States. The uniforms of the hotel staff, which differ widely depending on the staff member's function and which vary from season to season, remind guests of different periods in US history.

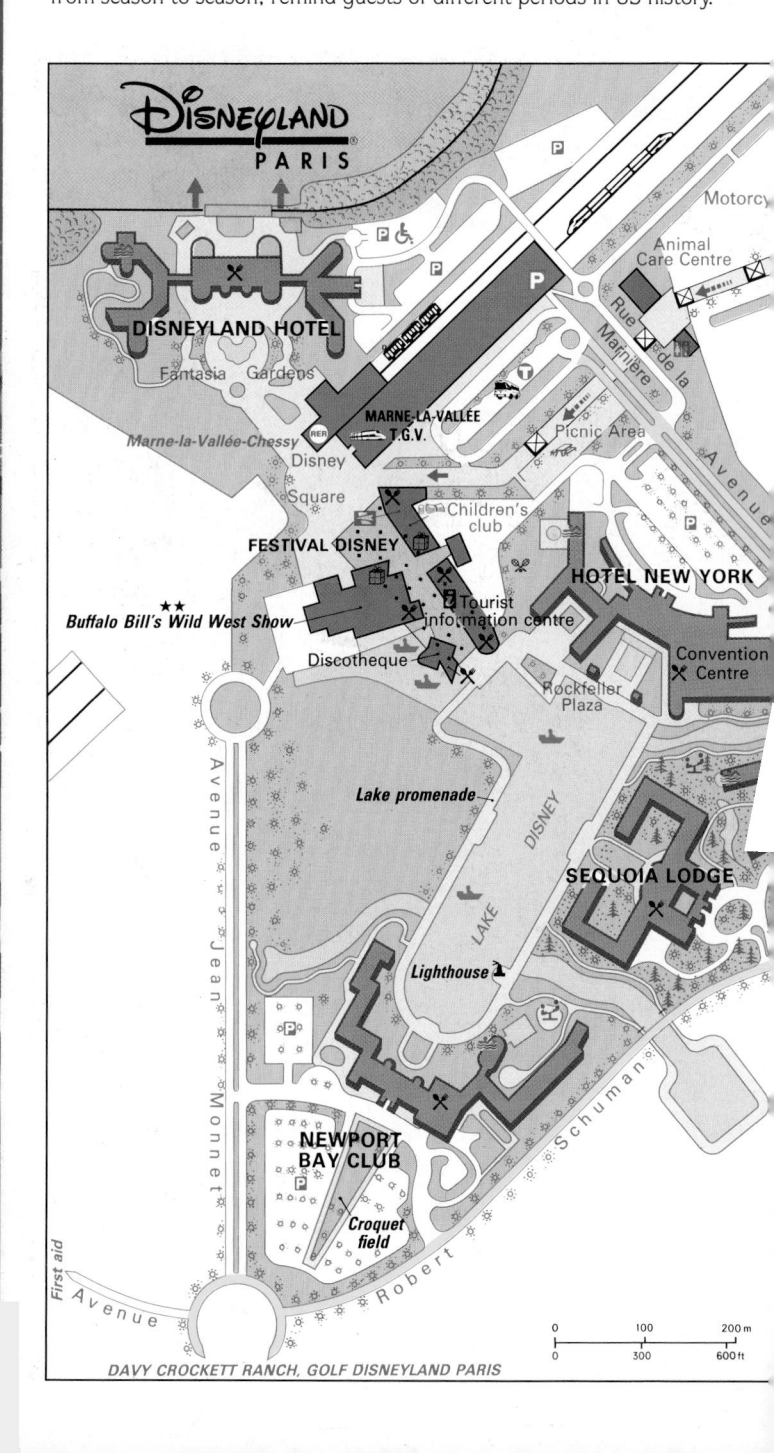

Goofy

Created in 1932, Goofy, the dog, appeared in 84 films. He is a blunder-prone source of unwitting humour.

Donald Duck

The irascible duck was introduced in 1934. He is a perpetual but soft-hearted grumbler, which explains his sometimes surprising reactions. A typical dreamer, his plans usually go awry.

Daisy Duck

She first appeared in a 1937 cartoon *Don Donald*.

Huey, Dewey and Louie

Donald's nephews were created in 1938. They are mischievous, reckless, smart, and very endearing. As Junior Woodchucks they are well-behaved and obedient.

Dumbo

The baby elephant with the aeroplane ears first appeared on the screen in 1941. He was taught to fly by Timothy the mouse. He counts many birds as friends.

Scrooge McDuck

First seen in 1947, richer than Croesus, this shrewd duck amasses mountains of gold and dollars, but his miserliness causes him nothing but trouble.

Chip'n'Dale

These two cheeky and sharp-witted chipmunks were created in 1943. Chip with a black nose and Dale with a red nose will do anything for hazelnuts.

Your favourite Disney characters are waiting to greet you "in person" throughout the day at Disneyland Paris; you can shake their hand, get them to sign your autograph book, and even have your photo taken with them!
If you fancy breakfast in their company, hurry along to Plaza Gardens Restaurant (Main Street USA) as soon as the park has opened. Minnie Mouse takes afternoon tea in front of the Château de la Belle au Bois Dormant, while Mickey himself can often be found near Casey's Corner.

Whether the visitor arrives by car (car park with some 11 500 spaces), bus or by public transport (RER/SNCF station), the entrance to the theme park is through Fantasia Gardens and past the luxurious Disneyland Hotel. There are several ticket booths and exchange booths (for foreign currency exchange). Disabled visitors have a separate car park for wheelchair access.

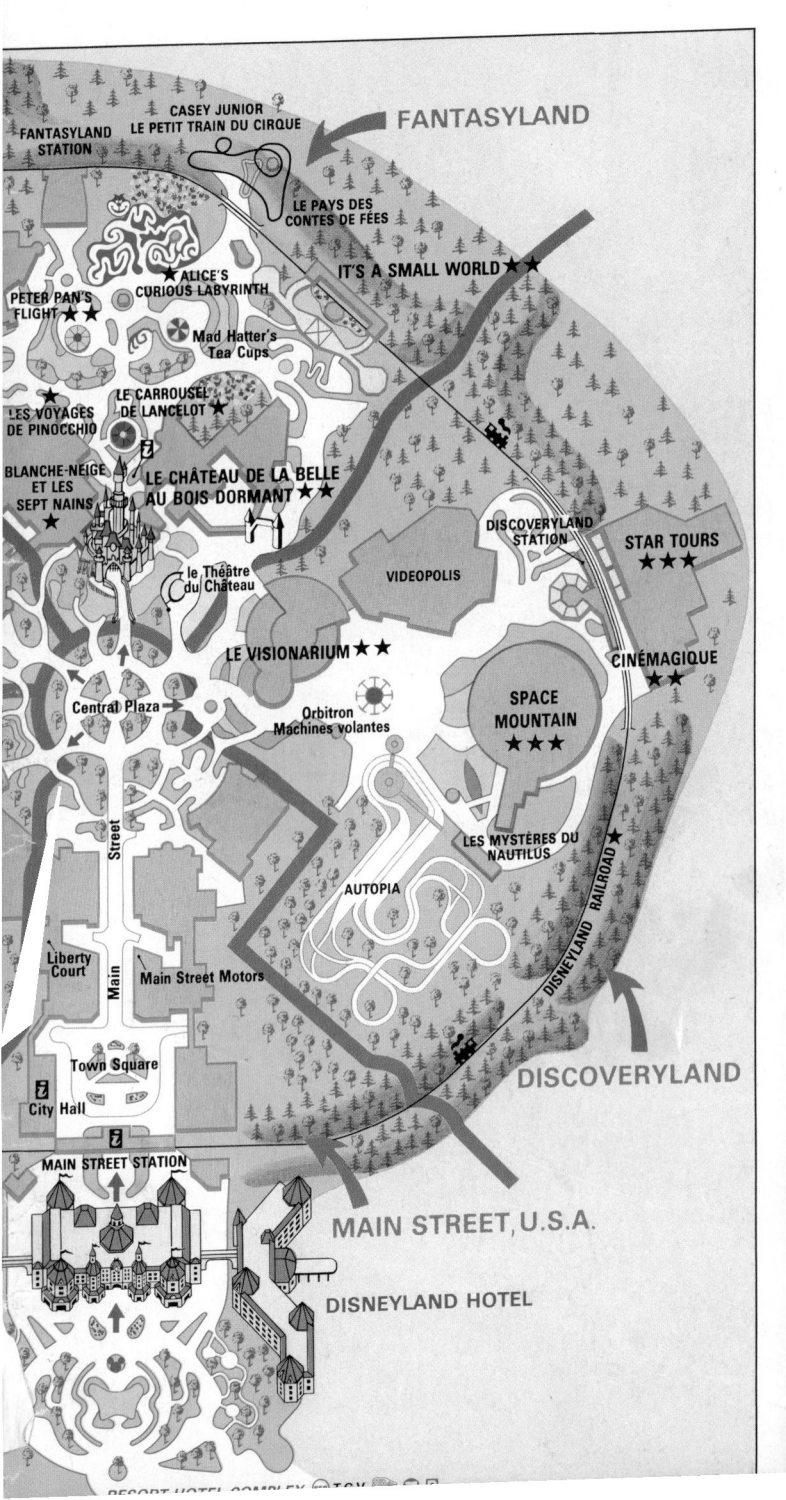

Luxury Class - 479 rooms, 21 suites

This five-storey luxury class hotel reflects the style and atmosphere of a turn-of-the-century grand hotel. This type of hotel was found in the top American seaside resorts where sea-bathing was enormously fashionable. The rich and famous resided in palatial establishments carefully attended by a very efficient staff. Splendidly equipped rooms and suites, plush salons and superb cuisine left the guests with indelible memories. Disneyland Hotel perpetuates this tradition.

The hotel's central building has a symmetrical construction with multi-facetted pink pavilions crowned by a dark red roofscape – a composition of infinite variety where pinnacles, gables, dormers and cupolas jostle for position. Glazed-over passageways lead to the two wings. As cars drive up to the grand entrance porch, they are greeted by the car attendant, resplendent in pink breeches and white collar and cuffs, who hastens to open the car door. Inside, a magnificent staircase leads from the spacious, elegantly appointed entrance lobby up to the rooms and restaurants. The lobby is dotted with armchairs arranged around coffee tables adorned with bowls of flowers. An enormous chandelier sheds light overhead.

Guests in the Castle Club have their own private entrance and receive personalised service.

All Disneyland Hotel guests have access to the health club, indoor swimming pool, sauna, jacuzzi and video games arcade.

Newport Bay Club

Moderate Class - 1 083 rooms, 15 suites

Located on the south side of Lake Disney, the Newport Bay Club borders a small curved bay, overlooked by a lighthouse. Named for the renowned resort of Newport, Rhode Island, the hotel evokes a prosperous early 1900s establishment true to the tradition of New England hospitality. The hotel buildings have an attractive colour scheme of pale grey and cream-coloured walls and grey-green roofs. An imposing 70m-233ft long colonnaded front overlooks the green expanses of carefully tended lawns.

The hotel has a part-indoor and part-outdoor swimming pool (Nantucket Pool), a health club, a sauna, a jacuzzi and a video games arcade.

There is a free bus service to the theme park and *Festival Disney*.

Hotel New York

First Class - 539 rooms, 36 suites

This hotel evokes several Manhattan neighbourhoods: Rockefeller Center, with five eight-storey tower buildings, Gramercy Park with its town houses and the East Side with its brownstones (brown-stone town houses built during the second half of the 19C); the town houses and brownstones form two wings flanking the towers.

The ornamental pool with fountain, on the lakeside, doubles as an ice-skating rink in winter. In addition the hotel has outdoor tennis courts, a half-outdoor and half-indoor swimming pool, a health club, a sauna, a jacuzzi and a video games arcade.

There is a free bus service to the theme park and *Festival Disney*.

Sequoia Lodge

Moderate Class - 997 rooms, 14 suites

Sequoia Lodge, with its long low lodges and stone facades, enjoys an appropriately landscaped setting overlooking Lake Disney. Its immediate environment reflects the Great American national parks and their woodland expanses, such as the Sequoia National Park in California. Many of these parks, which consist of vast stretches of forest, are home to a variety of species of which the most impressive are the giant sequoias that can live to be several thousand years old. The facilities include a part-indoor and part-outdoor swimming pool, a health club, a sauna, a jacuzzi and a video games arcade.

There is a free bus service to the theme park and *Festival Disney*.

Main Street, U.S.A.

The journey into make-believe begins. Main Street, U.S.A., the main street of an American town at the turn-of-the-century, is your first contact with the magical world of Walt Disney.
In the distance, at the end of the street, the graceful outline of Le Château de la Belle au Bois Dormant can be seen.
Streetcars drawn by brawny horses with liveried drivers, a double-decker bus, a Paddy wagon, a fire truck and a gleaming vintage limousine take young and old from Town Square up Main Street to Central Plaza, while the sound of brass bands and colourful orchestras floats through the air.
Main Street is lined with restaurants and shops, whose Victorian façades reflect an America of bygone days: Ribbons & Bows Hat Shop (for hats), The Storybook Store (for books, records and cassettes) and the Emporium (for clothes, souvenirs and toys) to name a few. This feeling of going back in time is further enhanced with street furnishings, including shop signs, gas lamps, street lights, fire hydrants and post boxes. Discovery and Liberty Arcades are two shop-lined arcades running parallel to Main Street. In addition to the shops they feature exhibitions on the inventions of man and the Statue of Liberty. Crowds gather every day to see the Disney parade, with floats displaying a host of familiar characters from the most famous Disney cartoons.

© Disney/Amblin Entertainment

√ Main Street Station

All aboard, please!
The **Disneyland Paris Railroad★** train, composed of five carriages pulled by an authentic steam locomotive, sets out from Main Street Station for an entertaining ride round the Disneyland theme park, with stops at **Frontierland, Fantasyland** and **Discoveryland.**
En route, a five-tableau **diorama** depicts the magnificent scenery and wildlife of the American **Grand Canyon.**

Dapper Dan's Hair Cuts

Straggly hair and stubbly chins are no problem for the barber in his 1900s-style barber shop with its comfortable tilt-back chairs and period posters. Take the time to have an old-time shave or haircut.

Main Street Motors (Vintage cars)

An old-fashioned petrol pump on the pavement outside marks the entrance to this "garage", now a clothes and sports wear shop. Two vintage cars are on display – a 1908 EMF convertible and a 1911 Oakland – and visitors can have their photo taken in front of them in period costume. Original posters, number plates and various mechanic's tools are included in this exhibition on

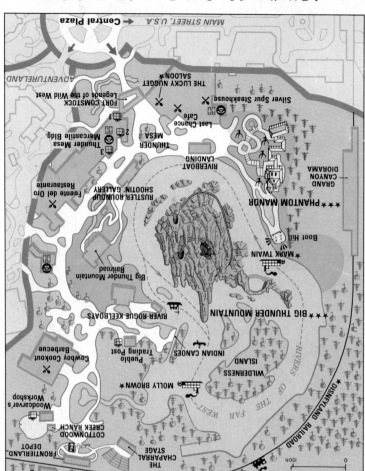

Map legend: 1 *Tobias Norton & Sons Frontier Traders* – 2 *Bonanza Outfitters*

Map labels:
← Central Plaza | MAIN STREET, U.S.A.
ADVENTURELAND
THE LUCKY NUGGET
FORT COMSTOCK Legends of the Wild West
Silver Spur Steakhouse
Last Chance Café
THUNDER MESA
Thunder Mesa Mercantile Bldg.
Fuente del Oro Restaurante
RUSTLER ROUNDUP SHOOTIN' GALLERY
RIVERBOAT LANDING
GRAND CANYON DIORAMA
★★★ PHANTOM MANOR
Boot Hill
★ MARK TWAIN
Big Thunder Mountain Railroad
★★★★ BIG THUNDER MOUNTAIN
RIVER ROGUE KEELBOATS
RIVERS
INDIAN CANOES
Pueblo Trading Post
WILDERNESS ISLAND
★ MOLLY BROWN
Cowboy Cookout Barbecue
Woodcarver's Workshop
COTTONWOOD CREEK RANCH
THE CHAPARRAL STAGE
FRONTIERLAND DEPOT
OF THE FAR WEST
DISNEYLAND RAILROAD
50 m / 150ft
0 / 0

River Rogue Keelboats

Two keelboats (these oddly-shaped boats travelled along the American waterways in the 18C), the *Raccoon* and the *Coyote*, set out from **Smuggler's Cove** on the same course as the riverboats.

Indian Canoes

Paddle your canoe, under the assistance of two trappers, along the Rivers of the Far West past abandoned mining operations, under rock formations and through wilderness caverns cut from Big Thunder Mountain.

The Chaparral Stage

Don't miss the Hillbilly Hoedown show *(consult the entertainment programme for times)*: country and western music and dancing, in which Chip'n'Dale can be seen in Stetsons, joined by Davy Crockett and the huge Hillbilly Bears.

Cottonwood Creek Ranch

At the entrance to this western ranch, in the **Woodcarver's Workshop**, a craftsman carves wood into animal shapes. In **Critter Corral** children will be delighted by animals, such as goats and sheep, which are tame enough to be stroked. Ducks and chickens strut (or waddle) about at liberty.

Frontierland Depot

This is an authentic Far West railway depot, with its goods shed and water tower. A pot-bellied stove warms up the station, where timetables and railroad maps tacked on the walls give information for departures aboard the Disneyland Paris Railroad. The train master's office, with its telegraph and ticket counter, is straight out of a vintage Western. The whistle toots, all on board the Disneyland Paris Railroad train – next stop, Fantasyland.

Disney theme parks

California: Disneyland

Disney's first theme park was inaugurated on 17 July 1955. The park covers 30ha - 74 acres and eight distinct lands: Main Street, U.S.A.; Adventureland; New Orleans Square; Critter Country; Frontierland; Fantasyland; Tomorrow-land and Mickey's Toontown. The Disneyland monorail links the theme park to the Disneyland Hotel and its three towers.

Florida: Walt Disney World Resort

This immense holiday complex covers over 11 000ha - 27 170 acres. On 1 October 1971, the **Magic Kingdom**, a new theme park, opened for business. Main Street, U.S.A.; Adventureland; Frontierland; Liberty Square; Fantasyland; Mickey's Birthdayland and Tomorrowland are spread over 43ha - 106 acres. **EPCOT Center** opened in 1982. Looking towards the future (Future World) with its exhibits on technological progress, this park also includes the World Showcase, which illustrates many different countries (Mexico, Norway, China, Germany, Italy, United States, Japan, Morocco, France, United Kingdom and Canada). 1989 saw the opening of **Disney-MGM Studios** (a park devoted to Walt Disney's productions), **Pleasure Island** (restaurants, shops and discos) and **Typhoon Lagoon** (a water theme park).
In addition to these recreational facilities there are also several themed hotels, a campsite, six golf courses and a mall with restaurants and stores (Disney Village Marketplace).
All of the components of the Walt Disney World Resort are linked up by bus, boat and two monorails. One of the latter runs right through the immense entrance hall of the Contemporary Resort Hotel.

Japan: Tokyo Disneyland

Opened on 15 April 1983, this park (46ha - 114 acres) like its predecessors covers several lands: World Bazaar with its covered shopping complex, Adventureland, Westernland, Fantasyland and Tomorrowland.

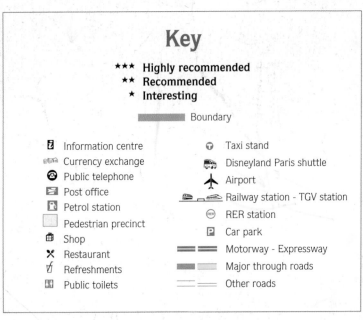

Key

*** **Highly recommended**
** **Recommended**
* **Interesting**

━━━ Boundary

🄓 Information centre
Currency exchange
🕾 Public telephone
✉ Post office
⛽ Petrol station
　 Pedestrian precinct
🏛 Shop
✕ Restaurant
Refreshments
🚻 Public toilets

🍽 Taxi stand
🚐 Disneyland Paris shuttle
✈ Airport
🚆✈ Railway station - TGV station
(RER) RER station
P Car park
━━━ Motorway - Expressway
━━━ Major through roads
━━━ Other roads

MANUFACTURE FRANÇAISE DES PNEUMATIQUES MICHELIN
Société en commandite par actions au capital de 2 000 000 000 de francs
Place des Carmes-Déchaux – 63 Clermont-Ferrand (France)
R.C.S. Clermont-Fd B 855 200 507

© Michelin et Cie, Propriétaires-Éditeurs 1995
Dépôt légal mars 1995 - ISBN 2-06-701271-1 - ISSN 0763-1383

Printed in France 03-95-30 - Photocomposition : NORD COMPO à Villeneuve-d'Ascq
Impression : MAME à Tours

Illustration de la couverture par Alain SAGUEZ/Daniel SPILER

Discoveryland

Discoveryland is recognizable by the futuristic style of its architecture. It not only looks ahead to the future, but also pays its respects to the greatest inventions of past centuries.

A special place is reserved for such famous visionaries as Leonardo da Vinci, Jules Verne and H.G. Wells, who showed that imaginary creations could become real.

© Disney/Lucasfilm Ltd

✓ Le Visionarium★★

A voyage through time in this circular-shaped building... an extravaganza of light and sound presenting flying machines, all kinds of inventions and technological marvels.

A video screen lights up and the Timekeeper appears. While he speaks, 9-Eye, a tubby robot equipped with nine camera-eyes, enters. The inventions that revolutionised the world flash by on the screen: the motor car, the aeroplane, the telephone, electricity.

Next step into the time machine: a specially-designed room where, in spectacular Circle-Vision on a 360° screen, a film takes you on an action-packed journey through many European countries.

As you are surrounded by theatre screens the impression is staggering – a strong sensation of being off balance is experienced.

CinéMagique★★

Captain EO, a 3-D film filled with special effects, stars Michael Jackson and is directed by Francis Ford Coppola. The hero finds himself embarked on a helter-skelter interstellar adventure.

George Lucas and Francis Ford Coppola joined with Disney to produce this astounding festival of sight and sound.

✓ Videopolis

A huge 35m-115ft long airship, the **Hypérion**, floats at the building's entrance.

Inside, giant video screens project cartoon clips.

Consult the entertainment programme for details of the evening show.

✓ Orbitron – Machines Volantes

High over Discoveryland, at the controls of your own small spacecraft, pilot through the galaxy past planets and constellations.

✓ Autopia

Young and old alike may drive a stylish racing car through a futuristic landscape.

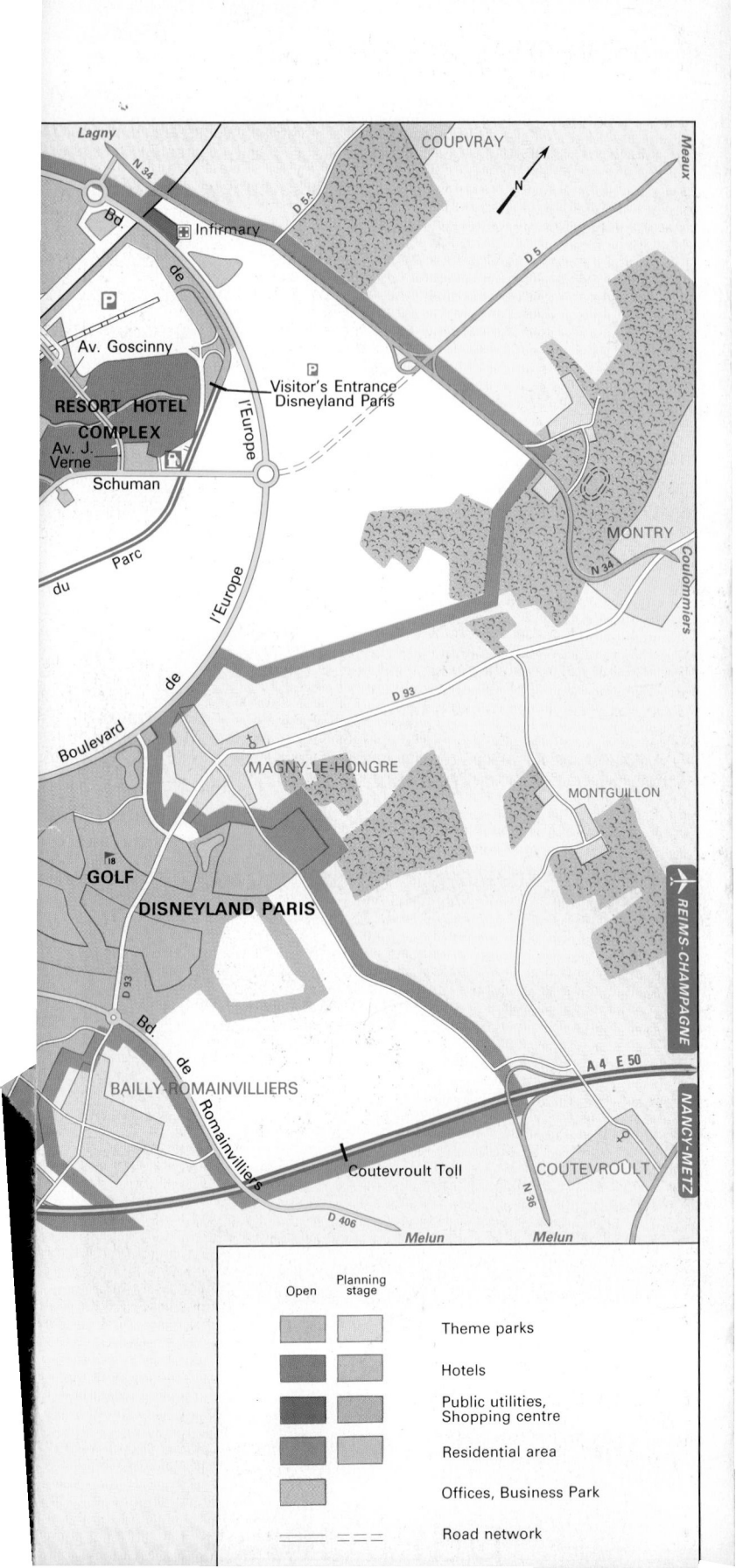

Lagny

COUPVRAY

N 34

D 5A

Bd

N

Infirmary

D 5

de

P

Av. Goscinny

l'Europe

Visitor's Entrance
Disneyland Paris

RESORT HOTEL
COMPLEX

Av. J.
Verne

Schuman

MONTRY

N 34

Coulommiers

Parc

du

l'Europe

de

D 93

Boulevard

MAGNY-LE-HONGRE

MONTGUILLON

18

GOLF

DISNEYLAND PARIS

REIMS-CHAMPAGNE

D 93

Bd.

A 4 E 50

de

BAILLY-ROMAINVILLIERS

Romainvilliers

NANCY-METZ

Coutevroult Toll

COUTEVROULT

N 36

D 406

Melun

Melun

	Open	Planning stage	
			Theme parks
			Hotels
			Public utilities, Shopping centre
			Residential area
			Offices, Business Park
			Road network

Practical information

Hotel and Camping Reservations

To reserve in one of the themed hotels or in the Davy Crockett Ranch:
– telephone: from the United Kingdom and Eire (01733) 33 55 65; in France
(1) 60 30 60 30.

Disneyland Paris Theme Park

Open all year from 09.00 to 18.00 (later in summer and school holidays).

Disneyland Paris Passports

One-day passport: in high season – adults and children age 12 and over 195F,
children from 3 to 11 years old 150F, free for children under 3; in low season – adults
150F and children 120F. Children under 7 years must be accompanied by an adult.
The day ticket gives one day's unlimited access to all the theme park's attractions
except the Rustler Roundup Shootin' Gallery (for which small change is needed).
Two-day passport (non-consecutive): in high season – adults 370F and children
285F; in low season – adults 285F and children 230F.
Three-day passport (non-consecutive): in high season – adults 505F and children
390F; in low season – adults 390F and children 310F.

Useful information

Suitable dress is required: shoes and shirts must be worn.
Disney information centre: City Hall (Main Street, U.S.A.).
Coin-operated lockers: Main Street Station.
Bank services: automatic teller machines (Main Street, U.S.A.).
Credit cards, Travellers Cheques in French Francs and Eurocheques are accepted.
Currency exchange: Main Entrance, Main Street Station, Frontierland Depot,
Adventureland and Fantasyland.
Lost and found: City Hall (Main Street, U.S.A.).
Camera rentals: both still and video cameras are available; apply at Town Square
Photography (Main Street, U.S.A.).
First aid: adjacent to Plaza Gardens Restaurant (Main Street, U.S.A.).
Public telephones: available throughout the theme park.

Children

Stroller rentals: Town Square Terrace (*30F plus a 20F deposit*).
Baby Care Center: changing tables and bottle warmers available adjacent to Plaza
Gardens Restaurant (Main Street, U.S.A.).
Lost children: Near Plaza Gardens Restaurant (Main Street, U.S.A).

Disabled

A brochure is available at City Hall (Main Street, U.S.A). Many of the attractions,
shops and restaurants are accessible to the disabled.
Wheelchair rental available inside the Main Entrance at Town Square Terrace.

Restaurants, cafés, delis...

Within the theme park there is a wide choice of self-service and table-service
restaurants offering a wide variety of fare from many different countries. Table-
service restaurants are licensed to serve alcoholic drinks with your meal.
Food and beverage carts serving pop corn, ice cream, bagels, potatoes, stir-fry and
ribs are set up throughout the theme park.

Animals

Pets, with the exception of guide dogs, are not allowed inside the Disneyland Paris
theme park or anywhere in the Disneyland Paris Resort. Pets may be boarded at the
Animal Care Center, located near the visitors' car park.

Picnic Area

A picnic area is located between the Disneyland Paris visitors' car park and Disney
Square. Food and beverages may not be brought into the theme park.

Post Office and Tourist Information Centre

Both are located in Festival Disney, the entertainment centre.

Star Tours★★★

While waiting for the space-ship to arrive, plunge into the turmoil of an orbital space station, a hive of activity where robots are repairing a star-speeder.

Then take a maiden voyage into space, aboard an interplanetary vessel piloted for the first time by a little robot, RX 24, known as Rex. Fasten your seat belts! Lovers of thrills will appreciate the headlong excitement of this sortie into space. The spacecraft lifts off, soars, dives, takes avoiding action, decelerates, manoeuvres to uncanny effect, as befits the work of *Star Wars* director George Lucas. This attraction, a favourite at other Disney parks, is outstanding for its flight simulation and special effects.

After the trip, visit the **Astroport Services Interstellaires** with its interactive video games.

Space Mountain★★★

This adventure in outer space was inspired by Jules Verne's novel *From the Earth to the Moon* (1873).

Daring would-be astronauts climb aboard little rockets which are fed into an enormous cannon, the *Columbiad*. Boom! You're off on a breathtaking supersonic journey through the cosmic wastes, trying to avoid meteorites, asteroids and other celestial bodies as you go!

Les Mystères du Nautilus (The Secrets of the Nautilus)

A bizarre metallic shape can be seen floating in the bubbling waters of a lagoon... this is indeed the *Nautilus*, the enigmatic Captain Nemo's submarine. The captain's voice welcomes passengers aboard. In the Grand Salon, Bach's *Toccata* is being played on the organ. Passengers can admire the depths of the ocean through the porthole. Suddenly an enormous tentacle appears... the submarine is being attacked by a giant octopus! Action stations!

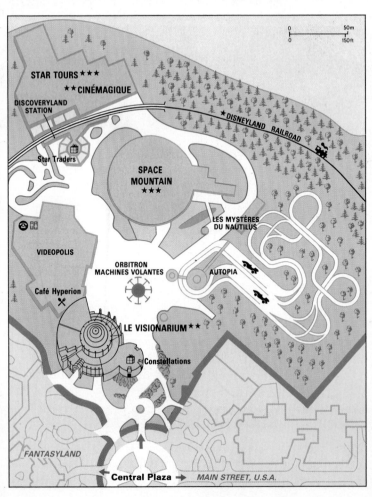

Disneyland Paris

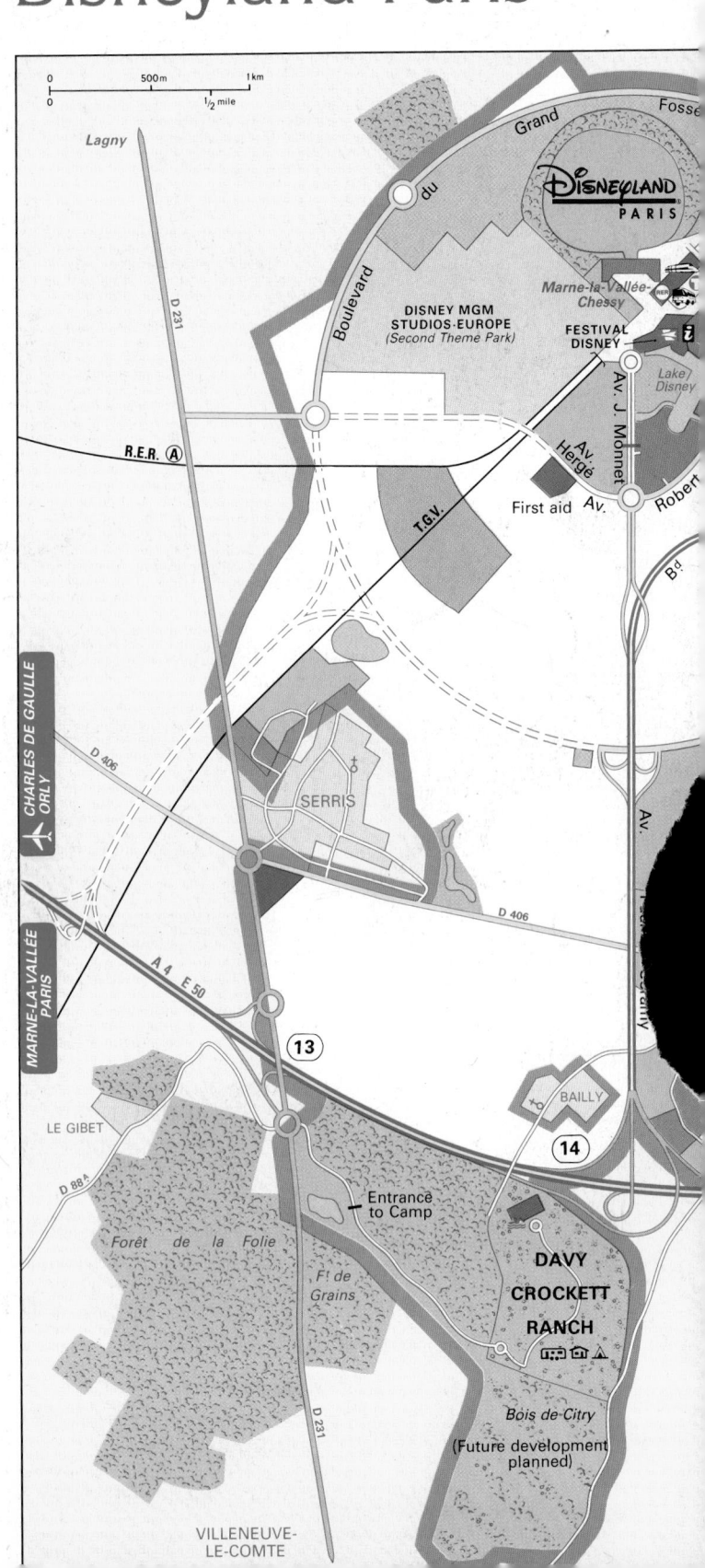

Lagny

Grand Fosse

DISNEYLAND PARIS

du

Boulevard

DISNEY MGM
STUDIOS-EUROPE
(Second Theme Park)

Marne-la-Vallée-Chessy

FESTIVAL DISNEY

Av. J. Monnet

Lake Disney

R.E.R. Ⓐ

Av. Hergé

Av.

First aid

Robert

D 231

T.G.V.

Bᵈ

✈ CHARLES DE GAULLE
ORLY

D 406

SERRIS

Av.

D 406

MARNE-LA-VALLÉE
PARIS

A 4 E 50

⑬

BAILLY

⑭

LE GIBET

D 88 A

Entrance to Camp

Forêt de la Folie

Fᵗ de Grains

DAVY

CROCKETT

RANCH

Bois de Citry

(Future development planned)

D 231

VILLENEUVE-LE-COMTE

0   500m   1 km
0   ½ mile

Mad Hatter's Tea Cups

This attraction is based on the Mad Hatter's Tea Party as recounted by Lewis Carroll in *Alice's Adventures in Wonderland*. Giant teacups whirl thrill-seekers on a wild ride.

Alice's Curious Labyrinth★

The visitor is confronted by many surprises as he wends his way through this topiary maze to the Queen of Hearts' Castle. Beware of the Queen of Hearts!

Le Pays des Contes de Fées (Storybook Land)

A peaceful little cruise with music in the background through scenes from Storybook Land, including *Snow White and the Seven Dwarfs*, *Hansel and Gretel*, *The Little Mermaid* and *Aladdin* among others.

Casey Jr, le Petit Train du Cirque (Casey Jr, the Little Circus Train)

All aboard for Storybook Land on Dumbo's beloved jolly little circus train.

✓ It's a Small World★★

Originally created for the 1964-65 New York World's Fair, this attraction is a tribute to the innocence and joy of children the world over.
Animated figures in national dress dance and sing in settings representing their homeland. The show's title song, sung in many languages, accompanie the boats that glide through this enchanted world of colour.

Fantasyland Station

The steam train pulls out from this Victorian London-style station and he for Discoveryland Station and then Main Street Station.

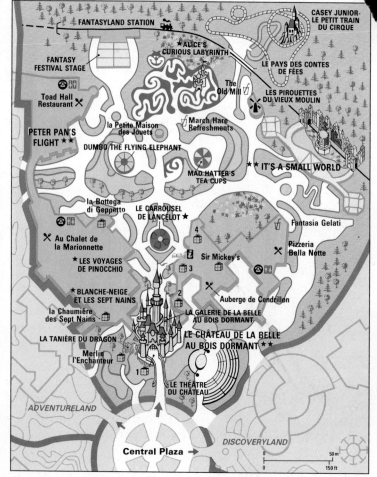

1 *La Boutique du Château* – **2** *La Ménagerie du Royaume* – **3** *Le Brave Petit Tailleur*

Fantasyland

Fantasyland is a make-believe world at the heart of Disneyland Paris. The wonderful land of European fairy tales (Grimm, Perrault and Carroll), as portrayed in the Disney animated classics, inhabits this quaint village with houses reminiscent of several European countries. You may run across Pinocchio, Alice in Wonderland, Snow White, Captain Hook and well-known Disney characters such as Mickey Mouse, Minnie Mouse, Pluto and Donald Duck, who will be delighted to pose for souvenir photos or give you their autograph.

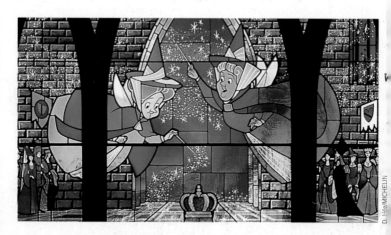

D. Hée/MICHELIN

Le Château de la Belle au Bois Dormant★★
(Sleeping Beauty Castle)

The castle with its turreted towers and gilded pennants dominates the theme park. Its architecture combines the features of a medieval fortress and a Renaissance château. In the **Galerie de la Belle au Bois Dormant** upstairs, tapestries, stained-glass windows and illuminated manuscripts recount the tale of Perrault's Sleeping Beauty. There is a marvellous view of Fantasyland from the castle ramparts. Down in the castle's depths, in **La Tanière du Dragon**, the dragon appears to be sleeping.

Blanche-Neige et les Sept Nains★
(Snow White and the Seven Dwarfs)

Mining cars from the dwarfs' mine carry young and old on a gripping journey through the enchanted forest. Beware, the Wicked Witch lurks everywhere!

Les Voyages de Pinocchio★ (The Travels of Pinocchio)

The puppet's adventures, based on the Italian Carlo Collodi's celebrated story *The Adventures of Pinocchio*, are recalled in this journey where we encounter Geppetto, Jiminy Cricket and the Blue Fairy, thanks to whom Pinocchio is turned into a real boy.

Le Carrousel de Lancelot★ (Lancelot's Roundabout)

Under a canopy detailing the heroics of Lancelot, 86 painted horses wait to take their riders on a joyous ride.

Peter Pan's Flight★★

Miniature pirate galleons take to the air for a flight over London and Never Land. A series of subtly arranged tableaux brings to life scenes from the Scottish author J.M. Barrie's play *Peter Pan* – the pirates' island, Captain Hook's brig, the rescuing of Princess Tiger Lily, the Indian dance, Captain Hook and the crocodile.

Dumbo the Flying Elephant★

With his winsome smile and upturned nose, Dumbo the baby elephant carries aloft all those who dream of soaring through the air.

Paris

From the huge Disneyland car park *(cars: 40F; motorcycles: 25F; caravans: 60F)*, sections of moving walkway take visitors most of the way to the theme park entrance.

Public transport includes the regional express network (RER) A line (the Torcy - Marne-la-Vallée line) from Paris (stations: Charles-de-Gaulle-Etoile, Auber, Châtelet-les Halles, Gare de Lyon, Nation) to Marne-la-Vallée and Disneyland Paris (station: Marne-la-Vallée - Chessy).

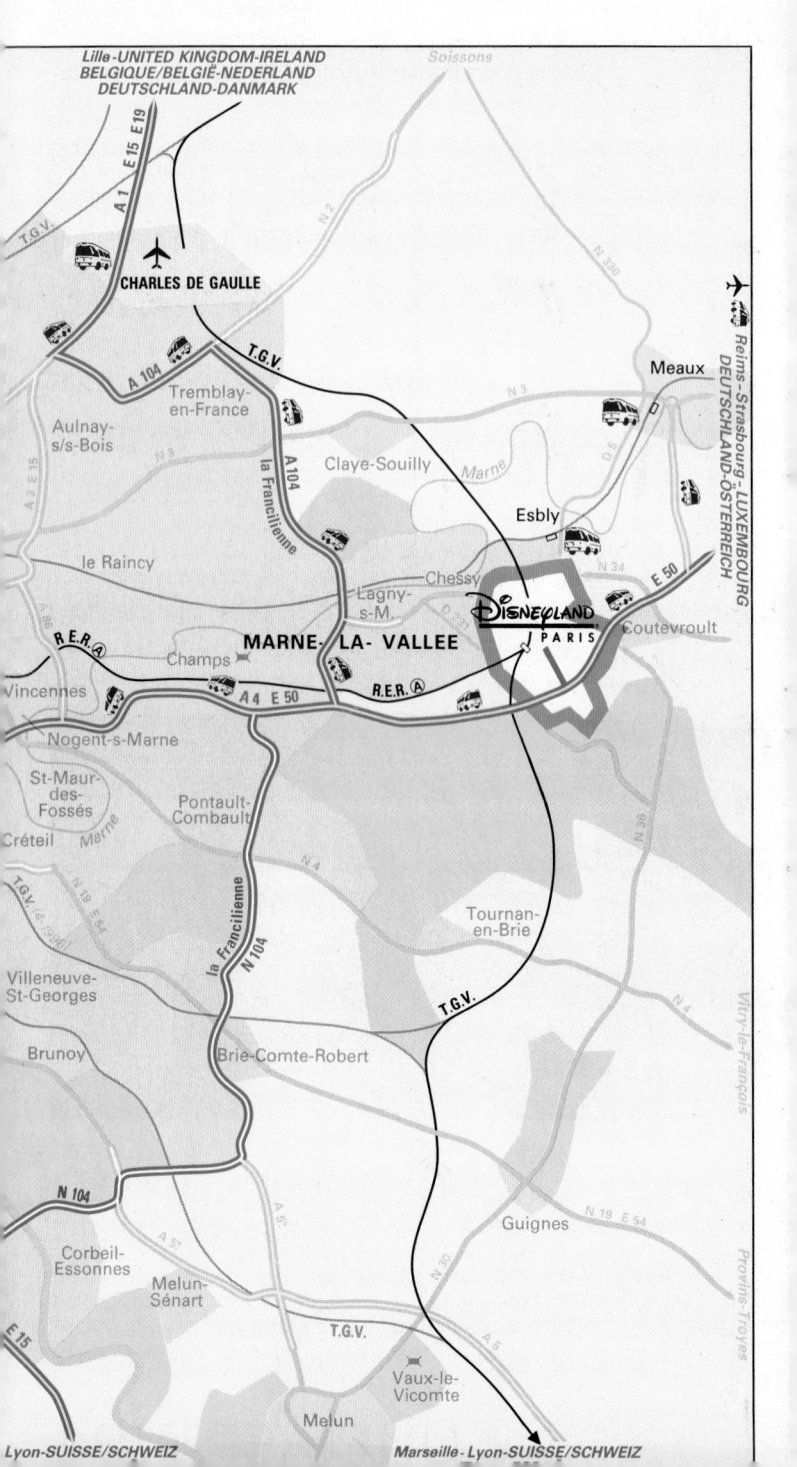

A stone's throw from

The map below indicates the extensive road network leading to Disneyland Paris.

The theme park and resort complex are located east of Paris and are easily accessible by motorway: A 4 (autoroute de l'Est) exit junction 14 *"Disneyland"*; the joint N 104 and A 104 (Francilienne) offers easy link up between the motorways A 1 (autoroute du Nord), A 6 (autoroute du Soleil) and, via the A 86, A 10 (l'Aquitaine) and the A 4 motorway.

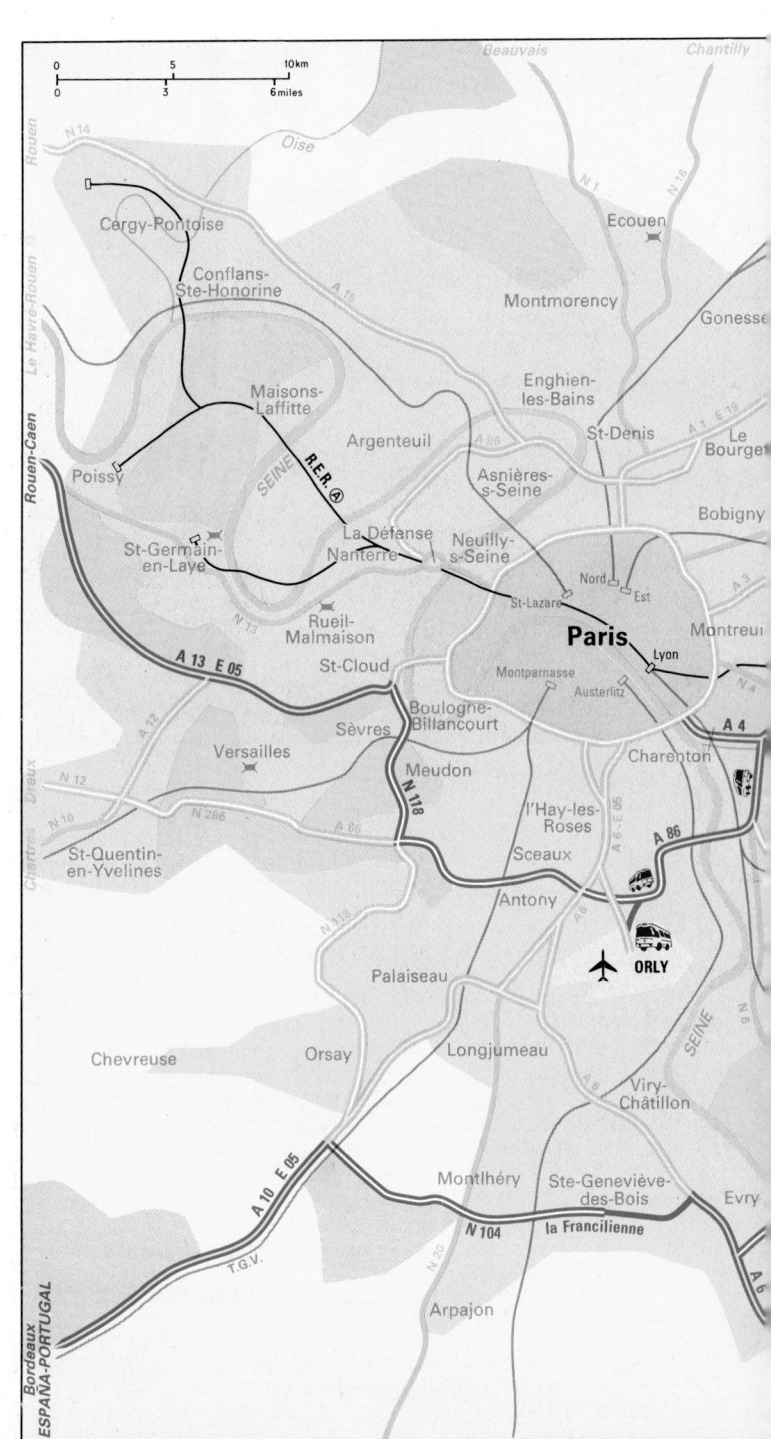

hapless prisoners try desperately to escape. In the harbour the pirate galleon fires salvo after salvo on the fort. The buccaneers plunder, pillage and carouse while the village burns and the arsenal explodes and becomes a burning inferno. This series of vividly enacted scenes is heightened by particularly ingenious special effects.

La Cabane des Robinson★★ (Swiss Family Treehouse)

From the isle in the middle of Adventureland, take the plank bridge to the neighbouring islet on which stands an enormous banyan tree.

The theme of this attraction is Johann David Wyss's novel *(Swiss Family Robinson)*, adapted for the screen in 1960 by Walt Disney. In the story a Swiss family, sailed for the New World from Le Havre. A violent storm caused their ship to founder. The parents and their three sons found themselves washed up on a desert isle, and fighting for survival.

The tree, which became their home, rises 27m-89ft above an elaborate maze of roots. The root cellar (Le Ventre de la Terre) is used both as a storage cellar and a place of refuge in time of danger. Climb the stairs to the top to visit the ingeniously furnished rooms of the family's new home.

Indiana Jones et le Temple du Péril★★
(Indiana Jones and the Temple of Doom)

A mysterious ruined temple… an archaeological dig with no signs of life… anyone brave enough to follow in the intrepid Indiana Jones's footsteps can climb aboard a little truck to find out more, but hold onto your hats during the ensuing crazy ride !

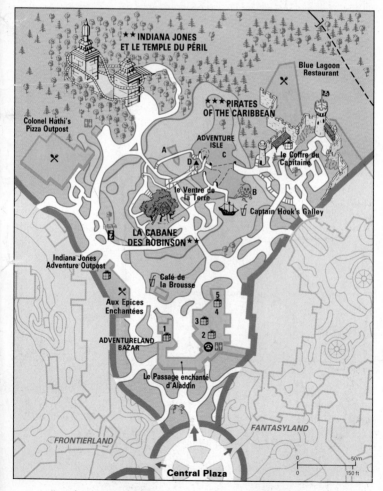

A L'Épave – **B** Skull Rock – **C** Ben Gunn's Cave – **D** Pirate Lookout
1 La Girafe Curieuse – **2** La Reine des Serpents
3 Les Trésors de Schéhérazade – **4** L'Échoppe d'Aladdin – **5** Le Chant des Tam-Tams

Adventureland

Beyond the exotic shops of Adventureland Bazar with their Arabian Nights atmosphere, is a land of mystery and enchantment.

Le Passage Enchanté d'Aladdin (Aladdin's Magic Passage)

Or, the story of how the street urchin from Agrabah was transformed into a handsome prince, not without one or two set-backs along the way…

✓ Adventure Isle

A mass of rock, lush vegetation, waterfalls, a shipwreck, a sinister skull, a pirate ship **(Captain Hook's Galley)** moored in Cannonball Cove, convey the island's mystery. Here, adventure and exploration go hand in hand.
What surprises are in store? Is there hidden treasure to be found in the labyrinth of subterranean grottoes leading to Ben Gunn's Cave?

✓ Pirates of the Caribbean★★★

The Caribbean – a word that conjures up tropical seas, treasure-laden galleons under full sail and… pirates.
In one of Disney's most celebrated attractions, the excitement of the Spanish Main lives again. Once aboard flat-bottomed boats visitors should prepare to relive high drama as a band of marauding pirates, animated by *Audio-Animatronics*® attack a coastal village and its fort. Watch out for those swashbuckling pirates and stray cannon-balls.

Europe

airports; shuttle buses operate from the 2 Paris airports. **By train:** after arriving at one of the following Paris railway stations (Gare du Nord, Gare de l'Est, Gare d'Austerlitz or Gare St-Lazare), take the métro to the A line of the **RER** at Auber or Châtelet-Les Halles stations or directly from the Gare de Lyon, to Marne-la-Vallée - Chessy station at Disneyland Paris.
Since 1994 the **TGV** high-speed train has had a stop at Disneyland Paris.

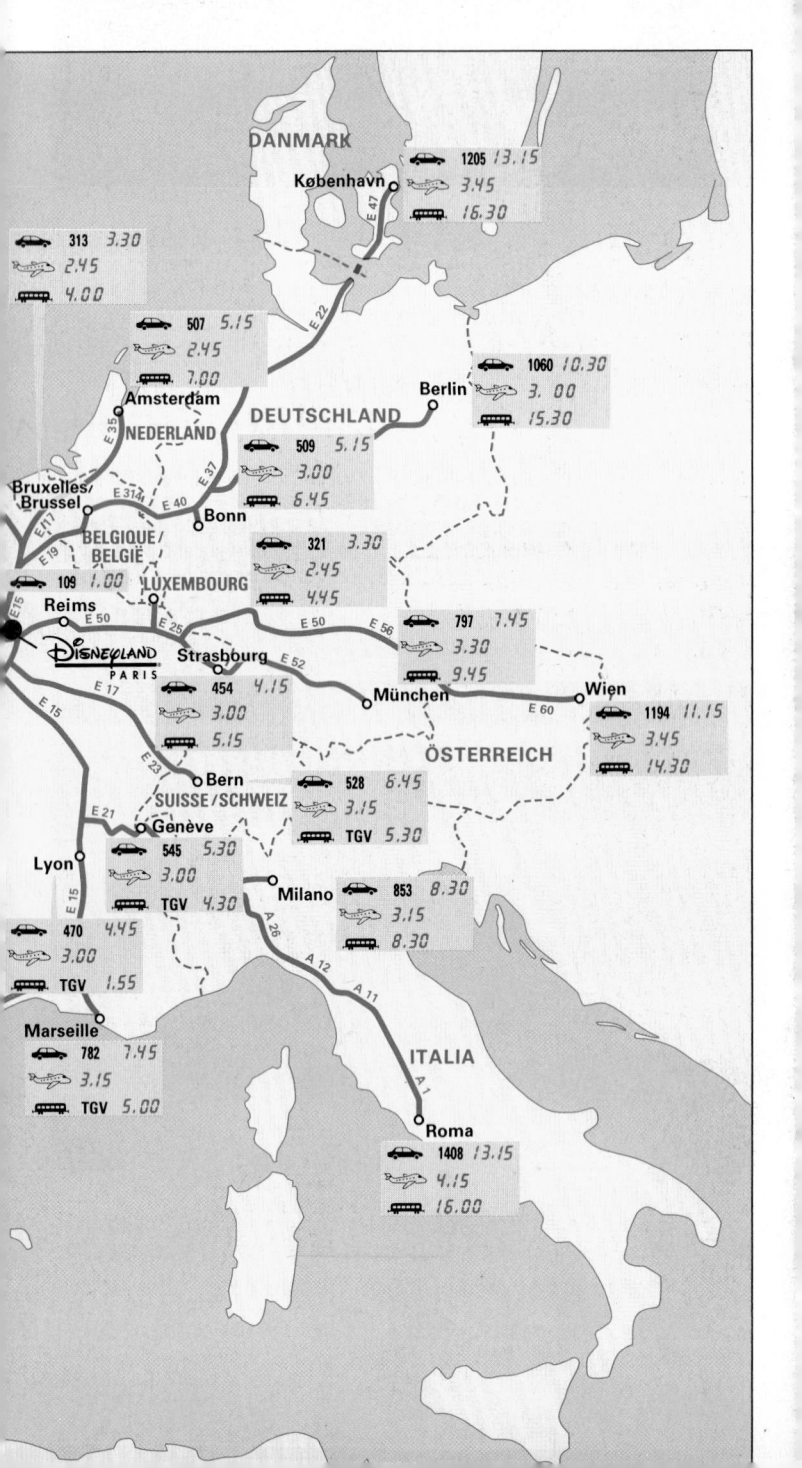

At the Crossroads of

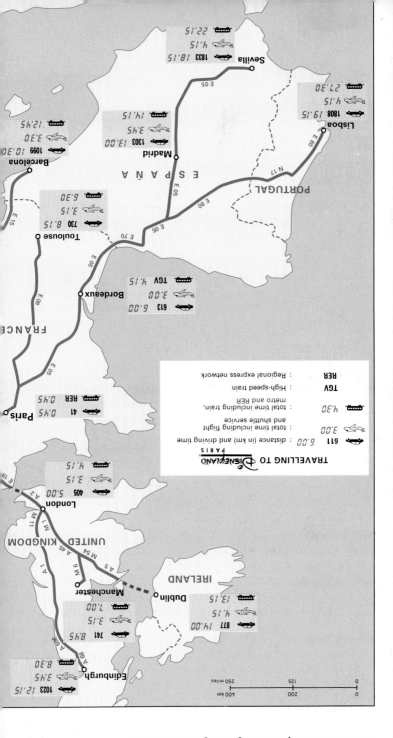

Because of its location some 30km – 20 miles east of the French capital, Disneyland Paris is strategically located on the Continent. The map below shows the **main routes** for travelling from the major European cities. The times shown with the kilometres are inclusive, that is, they indicate total travelling time from the city centres to Disneyland Paris; the same applies to the air and rail travel times. **By air:** to Orly, Roissy-Charles de Gaulle or Reims-Champagne

Walt Disney
a life devoted to enchantment

1901 On 5 December, Walter Elias Disney, the fourth child of Flora and Elias Disney is born.

1906 The family moves to a farm near Marceline, Missouri.

1910 The family leaves Marceline and settles in Kansas City. Walt, very early, shows an amazing talent for drawing.

1918 During the First World War, he joins the Red Cross and takes part in operations in France as an ambulance driver.

1919-22 After the war, he returns to Kansas City and draws for a small advertising studio. He meets a young Dutchman, Ub Iwerks, who shares his love of drawing. They become close friends and decide to pool their talent.

1923 Walt goes to Hollywood with $40 in his pocket. At the cost of much hard work, Walt and Ub complete a series of short films, called **Alice Comedies,** blending animation and live action.

1927 After Alice, Disney wants to invent a new, purely cartoon character; Oswald, the Lucky Rabbit, is created.

1928 Mickey and Minnie make their screen début in **Steamboat Willie,** on 18 November. This date marks a turning-point in Disney's cartoon technique and in his dazzling career.

1929 Creation of **Silly Symphonies,** cartoon shorts in Technicolor featuring animated animals, insects and plants. The *Skeleton Dance* is the first of 75 Symphonies produced.

1932 Disney was awarded his first Academy Award for **Flowers and Trees,** a cartoon in vivid colour. He receives an honorary Academy Award for the creation of Mickey Mouse, four years after his screen début.

1933 Success for **Three Little Pigs,** which wins an Academy Award.

1937-39 On 21 December, première at the Carthay Circle Theatre, Los Angeles, of the full-length animated feature film **Snow White and the Seven Dwarfs.** A triumph: Disney is awarded one full-sized Academy Award and seven dwarf-sized ones!

1940 Premières of *Pinocchio* and *Fantasia.*
The Disney Studios expand, employing over 1 000 people.

1941 *Dumbo* wins an Academy Award for Best Original Score.

1942 Première of *Bambi.*

1950 Disney produces his First Christmas Television Show. Success for *Treasure Island* (featuring live actors) and *Cinderella* (animated feature film).

1951 Première of *Alice in Wonderland.*

1954 The series *Disneyland* and *The Mickey Mouse Club* are children's firm favourites on American television. Release of the astonishing *20 000 Leagues Under the Sea.*

1955 **Disneyland,** the first theme park, opens in California.
Première of *Lady and the Tramp.*

1961-63 *One Hundred and One Dalmatians* and *The Sword in The Stone* are released.

1966 On 15 December, death of the man who spent his life turning dreams into reality. Faithful to Walt's ideas, Walt Disney Productions carry on his work.

1971 Inauguration in Florida of **Walt Disney World Resort,** with Magic Kingdom, the second theme park.

1982 Opening of **EPCOT Center** at Walt Disney World Resort.

1983 **Tokyo Disneyland,** another theme park, opens in Japan.

1989 Opening of **Disney-MGM Studios** at Walt Disney World Resort.

1990 *The Little Mermaid* is awarded 2 Oscars.

1991 *Beauty and the Beast* does well in the Academy Awards.

1992 12 April **Euro Disney Resort** opens east of Paris.
Release of Aladdin.

1994 Release of *The Lion King.*

It's show time

An entertainment programme with the times and whereabouts of the various shows (variable depending on the season) is available from City Hall (Main Street USA).

All year round, and in summer especially, there are numerous shows taking place at various points throughout the Disneyland Paris resort, in the theme park, Festival Disney, the hotels and Davy Crockett Ranch.

Buffalo Bill's Wild West Show

Festival Disney. The show captures the spirit of the Far West in the days of Buffalo Bill, with cavalcades, cowboys and Indians, stage coaches being held up etc.
Dinner show (as much beer and Cola as you can drink): 325F, 3-11 year olds: 200F.

La Parade Disney★★ and Main Street Electrical Parade★★

Fantasyland and Main Street USA. La Parade Disney is a day-time carnival procession (colourful costumes and lively music). Main Street Electrical Parade is an evening procession with illuminations (sparkling floats and costumes).

Fantasia in the Sky★ (Firework display)

Lake Disney. On a summer evening at the end of a magical day spent in Disney's world of fantasy the sky above Lake Disney bursts into a blaze of multicoloured flares and rockets. The fireworks are best seen from the banks of the lake, Fantasia Gardens or Main Street USA.

The Lucky Nugget Saloon★

Frontierland, **Lilly's Follies:** This musical revue is led with great aplomb by Miss Lil herself, the owner of this establishment, a saloon from the days of the Gold Rush. The saloon decor is inspired by the works of painters of scenes of the Far West such as Remington.

C'est Magique (It's Magic)

Fantasy Festival Stage (Fantasyland). A musical revue inspired by Broadway, with famous guest stars Mickey and Minnie Mouse, Donald Duck and Goofy.

Le Livre Magique de Mickey★ (Mickey's Magic Book)

Le Théâtre du Château (Fantasyland). Mickey appears in the costume he wore in *Fantasia* and opens a huge story book. Out of its pages spring characters from *Cinderella, Snow White and the Seven Dwarfs* and *Sleeping Beauty.*

La Belle et la Bête★★ (Beauty and the Beast)

Videopolis (Discoveryland). The fairy tale of the beautiful princess and the prince who was transformed into an ugly beast is brought to life in this marvellous show, with songs, dancing and splendid costumes.

Atmosphere Talent

Thirty or so groups of various artistes put on performances all year round in Festival Disney and the theme park, including music, dance, comic sketches, acrobatics etc.
– **Festival Disney:** jugglers, acrobats, people on stilts.
– **Main Street USA:** music from the early 1900s (jazz, Dixieland, ragtime).
– **Frontierland:** sketches and music from the American Far West. Cardplayers, beware... the Card Shark is on the prowl! Country and western music; Dixieland music on the Thunder Mesa Riverboat Landing.
– **Adventureland:** for those with exotic musical tastes, the rhythmic beat of African drums and percussion instruments.
– **Fantasyland:** trumpet and trombone players.
– **Discoveryland:** as you wait to test your nerves on Star Tours or the Space Moutain, out-of-this-world creatures can be seen wandering about, or playing string or percussion intruments.

Disneyland
PARIS

ISBN 2-06-701271-1

MICHELIN®

1995/1996